Andrew J:
The Corgi Who Rescued Me

To Terry

Janet E. Sutherland

ISBN: 978-1-3299-7807-2 (sc)
ISBN: 978-1-4834-5529-7 (e)

Library of Congress Control Number: 2016911528

Because of the dynamic nature of the Internet, any web addresses or links contained in this book may have changed
since publication and may no longer be valid. The views expressed in this work are solely those of the author and do
not necessarily reflect the views of the publisher, and the publisher hereby disclaims any responsibility for them.

Any people depicted in stock imagery provided by Thinkstock are models, and
such images are being used for illustrative purposes only.
Certain stock imagery © Thinkstock.

Lulu Publishing Services rev. date: 7/22/2016

This book is dedicated to my family (especially sweet Ella and Maya, who inspired me to write this book); to Kevin, who was Andrew J's hero; and to Andrew J, who rescued me.

"Andrew J inspired me each day. I smiled every time I saw a picture of him. His demeanor made it appear as if was talking and motivating me to never give up.I will always treasure his friendship, I will never forget all he did to make all of us fight the struggles we have in our life."

-Kathy Mielnicki Smertene, a beloved friend of Andrew J

"Man's best friend is also his spiritual companion and counselor. Andrew J helped Janet in her time of great need in a way that teaches us once again to appreciate the love and intuition freely offered by our pets."

-The Rev. George D. Smith, Rector,
St. Mark's Episcopal Church, Glen Ellyn, IL.

"Andrew J. Sutherland was the first and best Corgi I have ever met! He was my downstairs neighbor and, when I finally got a dog of my own, Andy was among the first to welcome Wrigley to his new home. They were always excited to see each other and were delighted when they had a few moments to chase each other in Janet's yard or along Drexel Boulevard. He was a loving dog with a sweet spirit and Wrigley and I miss him much."

-Tawa Mitchell, Andrew J's and Janet's Chicago neighbor.

"Andrew J was an affectionate and loyal member of Janet's family. His companionship was a blessing and brought both joy and hope to each new day."

-Christine Loose, friend of Janet

"Most would say that the dog was the one rescued but in this case I think Andrew J rescued Janet."

- Sheri Billing, friend of Janet and Andrew J.

Acknowledgments

This book would not have been possible without the help of my uncle Bob Sutherland.

Special thanks to my parents, Donald and Marie Sutherland, and my cousin Emily Brewster for their support and encouragement.

I would like to express my deepest appreciation to The Brain Aneurysm Foundation, which has helped me and many other survivors in our healing processes.

My gratitude to the Ohio Valley Corgi Rescue group, which helped me adopt Andrew J and provides many corgis with homes.

Deep thanks to Dr. Sepideh Amin-Hanjani of the Department of Neurosurgery at the University of Illinois at Chicago, who offered medical support in the creative process of this book.

I thank the staff of the Lombard Veterinary Hospital for their never-ending care of and sympathy for Andrew J and their generous donation in honor of Andrew J to the University of Illinois Companion Animal Memorial Fund.

Andrew J:
The Corgi Who Rescued Me

Andrew J was sitting alongside a country road, staring out at a muddy field, wondering how he was going to find his way to a new home.

Andrew J was a sweet corgi with foxy features, soft brown ears, stubby white legs, and a short nubby tail much like that of a bunny rabbit. He had a big heart, but he never seemed to be able to make his owner happy. He seemed to get yelled at for no reason, and sometimes he'd even get hit.

Today his owner had decided he didn't want to take care of Andrew J anymore. Sometimes dog owners do not understand how to take care of pets, show them love, or treat them as members of the family. The man had left Andrew J on the side of the road and driven away.

Poor Andrew J didn't know what to do or where to go. He started walking, but his leg hurt, and he was sore from being hit by his owner. His thick white and brown fur was soaking wet. His white paws were muddy, and he was very sad.

Fortunately, a nice couple drove by and saw him limping along the road. They pulled their car over and called to him. At first he was scared. *Are these nice people?* he wondered. He was afraid they would be mean like the man who had abandoned him, but he was so cold and scared that he let them pick him up and put him in their car.

They brought him to their house, where they took a warm towel and cleaned his muddy paws and talked to him quietly. "We'll help you," they said.

They gave him a warm soapy bath, which Andrew J did not like very much. Water was in his ears, and so was soap! He shook the water off and tried to run out of the room, but the nice lady caught him and wrapped him up gently in a towel. Finally, Andrew J was warm and clean, but his belly was growling.

Andrew J was hungry. *What's for dinner?* he wondered as he ran around this new house, following the couple into the kitchen. *Maybe they'll give me a cheeseburger and French fries*, he thought. *That would be yummy for my tummy!*

It turned out to be regular old dog food, but that was okay too.

Andrew J was very happy after dinner, so he lay down on the carpet on his back and wiggled back and forth with his clean white paws flopping around. This was his "wiggly smiggly" time. He had a big grin on his face and couldn't wait for more food. *Treats! Treats! Treats!*

Even though he didn't have a burger and fries, he was happy to be able to roam around this warm home, looking for a place to nap. Maybe the sofa? The nice couple put a Chicago Bears blanket on the floor for Andrew J. He thought, *This looks nice and cozy.*

He curled up and fell asleep with his tongue sticking out of his mouth. Andrew J dreamed he was chasing rabbits, and his paws and nose wiggled as he slept.

When he got up the next day, Andrew J sat outside in the backyard and watched the goldfish in a pond that was surrounded by stones.

Every so often, he would raise his paw and tap the water in hopes of catching a snack. He liked this new place!

The nice couple trained therapy dogs and seeing-eye dogs, so without realizing it, Andrew J was also learning to be a special doggy friend to people who didn't feel well. He was learning how to watch out for people who have been sick. Andrew J realized his new job would be taking care of people! He was also trying hard to be a great watchdog. *If I help out, I'll get more treats. Treats! Treats!* thought Andrew J. *Yummy for my tummy!*

* * *

When spring arrived, it was time for Andrew J to go on a new adventure. He loved going for car rides. He hung his head out of the window, his ears and gums flapping in the wind. Sometimes he sneezed because the wind was blowing up his nose. *This is fun!* he thought.

He wiggled his stumpy tail and bounced around the car. He wasn't sure where they were going. *But maybe there will be treats*, he thought. *Treats! Treats! Treats! Yummy for my tummy, yummy for my tummy*, he sang to himself as he bounced in the car.

Soon the car stopped at a cute little cottage with a front porch that was filled with colorful flowerpots. There were lots of trees, and he could hear birds chirping. Andrew J hopped out of the car. He bounced up and down, thinking, *More fun, more fun!*

The front door opened, and Andrew J got his first glimpse of Janet, a pretty lady with red hair and lots of sparkly jewelry. She called out his name, and he ran up the stairs and into the front hall and jumped right up on her. He looked up at her with his big brown eyes. It was love at first sight.

Janet sat down on the floor with him, rubbed his belly, and said, "Who's my tiny boy? Who's my sweet Andrew J?"

He loved this. Andrew J and Janet snuggled and played for a long time, and then she said the magic words: "Would you like a treat?" He answered yes by putting out his paw to shake her hand.

She had a special dog bowl and lots of treats that she called cookies. He sang to himself, *Yummy for my tummy, yum.*

The nice couple decided that Janet and Andrew J made a perfect match. Andrew J was a rescue dog and needed a forever home, and Janet needed someone to help take care of her and be her protector. The nice couple was so sad to leave, but they knew that this was the perfect place for sweet Andrew J.

Andrew J sat at the door for a long time, waiting for them to come back. Janet knew he was going to miss the wonderful couple, but she hoped he would love his new home with her.

That first evening in his new home, Andrew J was scared and lonely. Janet thought he needed extra love, so they cuddled up together on the floor. She told Andrew J that they would be a team. He would take care of her, and she would take care of him as well. Suddenly, he felt like he could conquer the world!

Janet showed Andrew J his new dog bed. *It's okay*, thought Andrew J. But then Janet told him he could sleep on her bed. He loved this. He climbed over the pillows and dug a fort under the sheets and blanket. He took over half the bed and fell asleep happily with his tongue hanging out of his mouth.

Later, Janet picked him up and tucked him into his own bed, singing, "Momma's baby boy, Momma's Andrew Joy." He pulled his paws up underneath his nose and snored, dreaming of squirrels and treats, treats, treats!

Janet and Andrew J became fast friends. Every morning, Andrew J would stretch and yawn really big and make a noise. He would blurt out a little sneeze and do his little "wiggly smiggly," rubbing his back on the carpet and smiling, with his head pointed up to the ceiling.

Janet sometimes had trouble walking because she was still recovering from an illness. Before Andrew J came to live with Janet, she had suffered a brain aneurysm: a balloon on a blood vessel had burst in her head. She had spent a long time in the hospital while it healed.

She was better now, but sometimes her legs didn't do what she wanted them to do, and she was often very tired.

So each morning, Andrew J would wait for Janet at the bottom of the stairs to make sure she was okay. Once they ate breakfast, Andrew J would sit on the back porch and bark at the squirrels and scare the birds away. He thought he was protecting Janet. He also really loved doing it because he would eventually get treats, treats, treats!

Not long after Andrew J came to live with Janet, she decided to take him to a pet store to buy some new toys and treats. She put Andrew J in a shopping cart and pushed it into the store. He did not like this. It was scary with so many people, and there were other dogs running around. Andrew J could smell treats and animals, but this was a new place, and it brought back sad memories of being scared and not knowing where he was. He started shaking. Janet comforted Andrew J, and they left as quickly as they could. Both Janet and Andrew J realized that memories of scary times could go away if they learned to depend on each other. By taking care of each other, they would each feel safe and not sad.

Janet's friends all fell in love with Andrew J. They would scratch his ears and rub his head. They all thought Andrew J was a very special dog, which made him very happy. Andrew J loved to show off for his "girlfriends." He especially loved his squeaky orange football, and he would toss it in the air and hit it with his paw. Andrew J knew everyone was impressed.

Andrew J wasn't sure why Janet's friends called her "Zsa Zsa," but she sure loved pretty things, and she always smelled like flowers. Andrew J loved to see Janet smile, and he thought the sound of her laugh was almost as good as the sound of the treat jar opening.

The holidays were a special time for Janet and Andrew J. He loved getting new toys, but he wasn't so sure about all the costumes that were involved. At Christmas, he would wear antlers, and for Halloween he had a sparkly collar and pumpkin tie. For Easter, Andrew J wore bunny ears.

The tie is okay, but I'm not sure I like the bunny ears and the antlers, he thought. But it made Janet happy, and he always got treats, treats, treats!

The first time Christmas arrived, Andrew J was a bit confused because he didn't understand why Janet put a big tree with sparkly lights and red shiny balls in the middle of the living room. He did notice there was a long fuzzy sock with his name on it hanging from the fireplace mantle. *What could this mean?* he wondered. He tried to reach the stocking by jumping up, but his little stumpy white legs wouldn't get him up close enough to see inside of it. *Hmm, what is in that sock?* He would sit and stare at it every day.

Andrew J was able to sniff under the Christmas tree to explore the packages. He also knocked some of the ornaments from the tree because they had a yummy smell. Janet knew what he was up to because Andrew J always had glitter on his nose afterward.

Andrew J didn't like the snow very much. It was hard for him to get through the snow with his short little legs. But he knew Janet had trouble walking in it too, so he would try to make a path for her by pushing the snow out of the way with his nose.

One morning as they headed out on a walk, Janet surprised Andrew J by bringing out a red and gray velvet coat for him to wear. Janet put the coat over him and snapped it underneath his belly. *Oh no, not another silly costume*, thought Andrew J. *What is this thing?*

Janet took him outside, and he quickly discovered that the coat was keeping him warm. When he came inside, he knew it was time for treats and "wiggly smiggly" time! *Winter isn't that bad with this fancy coat*, he thought.

What a fun day! It was cold, but Janet took good care of Andrew J, and he barked at squirrels while wearing his fancy red velvet coat. Andrew J felt like he was in charge. He fell asleep that night dreaming about treats, treats, treats!

When spring arrived, Janet and Andrew J went out to take an afternoon walk around the neighborhood. The flowers were in bloom, and the ducks were quacking in a nearby pond. Andrew J saw how big those ducks were, and he sat, thought, stuck his little ears up, scooted closer, barked, and decided he needed to protect Janet from the ducks. Janet knew the ducks wouldn't hurt her, but it made her so happy to know that Andrew J wanted to protect her and keep her safe.

Sometimes Janet had trouble stepping up onto the street curb to get to the sidewalk, but Andrew J figured out a way to help her. He would step up on the curb first and then pull her up with his leash. It made him feel good to have such an important job to do! He would lick Janet's hand and sit by her side when they stopped to rest along the way.

For such a little dog, Andrew J had a big appetite. He could be sleeping in another room and wake up at the smallest sound of the treat jar being opened. One time he even came running when he heard a few grains of rice fall on the kitchen floor. He had great hearing.

Andrew J loved to take naps. He would stretch out on the floor with his legs straight behind him in the same position Superman uses when he flies. The Superman position allowed Andrew J to be ready to chase a squirrel or catch any crumbs that might fall on the floor—even when he was asleep.

For fun, Andrew J loved to run at top speed around furniture with a huge smile on his face. He knew there would be something waiting for him when he was done. *Treats! Treats! Treats! Yummy for my tummy, yum.*

Andrew J was just getting used to Janet's little house in the country when they decided to pack up the car and move to a big city. Janet introduced Andrew J to the heart of Chicago. She put Andrew J in the car, and he took his paw and opened the window so he could hang his head out and check out all of the people and cars. As they drove up and down Michigan Avenue, he barked at people, thinking, *I am in charge, and I'm going protect Janet from all of these people.* Andrew J wiggled his behind, and the fur on his back stood up.

Andrew J loved strolling the streets of Chicago. There was so much to explore! Andrew J's favorite place to sniff around was at Buckingham Fountain.

In the summer, he drank a bowl of water and had a little treat as he watched the fountain spray water into the air. Andrew J also loved Janet's friend Kevin, although it had taken him a little extra time to love Kevin because he was afraid of most men. Kevin understood that Andrew J didn't like to get wet, so he would protect Andrew J and take him around the fountain to explore all the interesting smells.

There were kids running around the fountain at night, waving lighted sticks at Andrew J, and he barked at them. He worried that the sticks might hurt Janet and Kevin. It was his job to protect his friends and make sure everyone knew he was in charge.

The end to a day always included "wiggly smiggly" time, and then he fell asleep with a smile on his face. He was a happy pooch: his belly was full, and Janet was safe.

Sometimes Janet was sad because she couldn't walk like she used to before her illness, but Andrew J had a way of making her sadness go away. He even helped other people who had injuries or who were in wheelchairs. Janet wondered if maybe he had once been trained as a therapy dog even before the nice couple found him. He certainly was therapy for her!

Andrew J's new home was in Hyde Park, where President Obama lived before he went to Washington, DC. One day, Janet walked Andrew J past the Obama family's house, and there were a lot of people with television cameras standing outside.

This Mr. Obama must be really important, thought Andrew J. Distracted by that thought, Andrew J stopped and lifted his leg on the grass to pee. Suddenly, the people with cameras came over and took pictures. *I'm famous!* thought Andrew J. But he also thought, *Oh, maybe this is not a good idea. Oops!* Janet let Andrew J have his picture taken, but when one of the camera people got too close to Janet, Andrew J barked at him. He thought, *I am a protector—stay away!*

Andrew J was actually a little scared by all the attention. Janet and Andrew J went back home for a belly rub and treats, treats, treats!

Boy, being a celebrity can be tiring, thought Andrew J. *It's time to nap. Too much excitement in the big city today!*

As much as Andrew J loved walking along the shore of Lake Michigan, he didn't like getting his paws wet. It reminded him of when he was sitting on the side of the road, scared and lonely. But Janet decided to show Andrew J one of Chicago's most beautiful beaches. Kevin put Andrew J in his car, and the three of them went to the beach. It was quite an adventure. *This sandy stuff is slippery to walk on, and I don't really like getting my paws dirty*, he thought. So he sat on a rock and tried to lick the sand off his paw. *Yuck!* It tasted terrible.

Janet liked to take Andrew J with her when she explored the neighborhood. It was kind of loud with sirens and car horns, but Andrew J loved the walk because there were lots of smells. One day Janet and Andrew J walked past a nursing home. Several men in wheelchairs were sitting outside, enjoying the beautiful day. Andrew J stopped and looked at the men. They smiled and reached out their hands to let Andrew J sniff.

Andrew J thought these men needed friends. *Maybe that will make them feel better*, he thought. Even though he was usually afraid of men, he felt like these were people who could use his help.

He was friendly to the men and very polite. Andrew J shook their hands by lifting his chunky paw up when they said, "Give me five, Andrew J."

He thought, *Boy, to be stuck in a wheelchair all day would be so hard.* This made Andrew J feel protective of his new friends. He wanted to be friends with these men because they needed his help. Andrew J thought back to when he was injured and muddy and probably looked very sad and lonely. He thought about the nice couple who rescued him.

Andrew J sat and looked at the men and then wiggled his tail and smiled at them.

They became his new friends, and he looked forward to visiting them each week. One day, Andrew J was out in the yard and saw one of the men coming down the sidewalk. The man called, "Andrew J, where are you?"

Andrew J ran over and greeted him. He wiggled his behind and bounced up and down. They were both so happy to see each other. Andrew J thought, *It's a great new life in Chicago, especially helping people who need it.*

Their new yard in the city was pretty and full of flowers and bushes. Some of the dogs in the neighborhood became Andrew J's friends. He especially liked Wrigley, a small white dog who lived down the street. There were also two tiny dogs who barked at Andrew J every time he went for a walk with Janet. Andrew J thought they were loud and silly, bouncing up and down when they barked. Janet called them the "yabadabadoos." He didn't need to protect Janet from those silly dogs.

Andrew J's best friend lived next door.

Ziggy was great fun! Ziggy had gray fur and a gray beard. He was younger than Andrew J, but they both enjoyed sitting in the front yard, barking at everyone who walked by and at any loud noises they heard. Ziggy and Andrew J knew they were protectors not just of their yard, but of the whole neighborhood.

When Ziggy was not outside to play, Andrew J would sit in the yard and wait for him and eventually bark at Ziggy's yard to try to get his attention. After a long day of barking and running around the yard, Andrew J would go inside. It was "wiggly smiggly" time as he rolled around on the floor, rubbing his back on the carpet and smiling.

When Janet had to leave for work in the morning, she would lean down to kiss Andrew J on the head, and her purse would accidentally hit him on the head. This happened almost every day, and it made Andrew J grumpy. *This is the frustrating part of being so short*, he thought.

On a very hot summer day, Janet seemed to be moving very slowly, and Andrew J really didn't like sitting outside so long in the heat. But Janet insisted they go outside so that she could pull weeds out of their garden. Janet was working hard to quickly get out of the heat.

Andrew J wanted to go inside, so he sat in front of the door, hoping Janet would let him in. It was just too hot. Suddenly, he saw her fall to the ground. She had fainted in the heat. She tried to yell out for help, but no one could hear her. Andrew J ran over and sat at her side and barked as loud as he could.

Eventually, some nice firemen arrived and helped Janet get inside the house to cool off. Andrew J followed Janet the rest of the day. He was worried about her. Andrew J sat at the foot of Janet's bed as she rested. She was better after a rest, but Andrew J thought, *I need to never leave her side, so she knows I am with her and will protect her.*

In late summer, another adventure awaited Andrew J! He and Janet moved to the suburbs to be closer to Janet's family. They needed a place full of parks and new friends. Andrew J loved the new home. Janet made sure it was cozy for him. He had a light blue snuggly bed in front of the window where he could watch the birds, squirrels, ducks, and deer. They took walks every evening. Andrew J would sniff near the stream where deer grazed and where ducks and their little babies swam and quacked. He knew this was a great place where he could watch over Janet.

One day, when Janet was leading Andrew J outside for a walk, they passed a mirror, and guess what he saw? Andrew J saw himself in the reflection! He thought, *Wow, I am a handsome boy!* After Andrew J discovered the mirror, he always made Janet stop so he could look at himself before they went out for a walk. And he would think, *Wow, I am still quite a handsome boy.*

Andrew J liked to sit and stare at the wildlife. Bunny rabbits sometimes ran behind Janet and Andrew J when they took walks. *This is sure different than the big city,* he thought. Andrew J felt like he was in charge of the entire community! Janet had trouble walking in the grass, so Andrew J would help her get through grassy yards. He would lead her away from holes and uneven ground so they could get home safely. He was the protector, and he knew that meant treats, treats, treats!

Summer was one big, long party at their new home. Andrew J sat outside all day and watched people swimming in the pool. He did not like water, but he enjoyed watching Janet and Kevin swim and get exercise.

When he got tired of watching, Andrew J would rest his head on the grass and wiggle his nose every time he heard the splashing water from the pool. *That water better not get near me. I don't want my ears or paws to get wet.*

Sometimes Andrew J didn't like sitting by the pool, so he would sit in the house instead, digging into the trash and eating tissues. Andrew J loved to munch on tissues and leave the pieces around the house. This didn't make Janet happy, but it certainly kept Andrew J amused.

After they were done in the pool, Janet and Kevin would come back to the house and cook dinner on the grill. Andrew J protected the grill by watching the juices from the burgers drip onto the floor. He thought, *Finally, I'll get my hamburger!* Kevin did make sure Andrew J got some burger yummies.

Kevin was Andrew J's good buddy. They sat together in the living room to watch football and took long walks together. Kevin let Andrew J sniff every tree and chase the squirrels and bunny rabbits, and then he gave Andrew J a nice big treat when they finished their walk. *Yummy for the tummy, yummy yum!*

After their walks it was "wiggly smiggly" time. Andrew J rolled around on the floor, happily rubbing his back on the carpet.

Andrew J could always sense when Janet wasn't feeling well, and at those times he worked extra hard to find ways to cheer her up and make her day easier. Sometimes he would just sit on her feet, snuggle up against her, and lick her hand. He knew that simple things like showing her love and affection would help. Janet loved Andrew J very much, and he loved her back.

When Andrew J was sore from too much playing, Janet rubbed his head, and he fell asleep with a smile on his face. When it was time for Janet to take her medicine and she was too busy working on her computer, Andrew J would jump on Janet and bump her until she stopped working and took her medication.

Janet's sadness slipped away whenever she and Andrew J found adventures, such as chasing squirrels, visiting Buckingham Fountain, and visiting their nice neighbor Peggy.

Peggy was a cheerful Irish woman who sat out on her porch swing every evening. She loved dogs and all animals. Peggy and Andrew J became great friends. She called Andrew J "AJ." Janet and Andrew J sat on the swing with Peggy and chatted in the evening. Her home overlooked a stream and there was a big weeping willow tree hanging over the water. It was a peaceful place.

Andrew J tried to climb the rocks by the stream to look for new smells. He sat in the green grass as the willow tree blew in the wind, and his ears flopped around as the summer breeze cooled him off.

When Janet broke her foot, Andrew J worked extra hard to help her get better. He slept next to her every night, with his head resting on her stomach. Andrew J forgot about treats. He just worried about Janet. She got better quickly because he was with her, snuggling, napping, and drooling on the pillow that they shared. Andrew J thought, *I am a true protector!* Andrew J gave Janet affection, never-ending love, and comfort. This helped her feel better and heal quicker.

Pets and people can help heal each other. Caring for Andrew J gave Janet a sense of purpose and helped her to not feel alone.

With Janet's help, Andrew J was able to forget his sad past, help others, and live every day joyously. Dogs like Andrew J have bigger hearts than anyone! Andrew J, the gentle protector, changed many people's lives and created a happier world.

There are millions of dogs just like Andrew J who are looking for a "forever home." Andrew J changed Janet's world, and Janet gave Andrew J a whole new adventurous life.

A portion of proceeds from the sale of this book will go to:

CorgiAid is a nonprofit organization founded to provide financial assistance to corgis and corgi mixes. The organization helps people who rescue dogs from shelters or other nonpermanent homes and who then foster them until a new home is found. Medical and other expenses for these dogs can become high; CorgiAid gathers donations from those who want to help and, following funding guidelines, provides funds to those rescuers who apply for help.

The Brain Aneurysm Foundation is the globally recognized leader in brain aneurysm awareness, education, support, advocacy, and research funding. The foundation provides support, educational materials, and information to brain aneurysm patients, their families, and the medical community. The Brain Aneurysm Foundation also funds essential research that can directly benefit those affected by brain aneurysms and that can help reduce the incidence of ruptured aneurysms. For more information, visit the foundation's website at www.bafound.org.

About the Author

Janet E. Sutherland is a former Chicago radio news reporter. In 2004, she became a brain aneurysm survivor. Sutherland met Andrew J while living in Dublin, Ohio, and she adopted him in 2005. Andrew J crossed the rainbow bridge in December 2015.